W9-AAT-753

Classification

Holly Wallace

Heinemann Library
Chicago, Illinois

© 2001 Heinemann Library
a division of Reed Elsevier Inc.
Chicago, Illinois

Customer Service 888-454-2279

Visit our website at www.heinemannlibrary.com

Designed by Celia Floyd
Originated by Dot Gradations
Printed in China

05 04

10 9 8 7 6 5 4 3 2

Library of Congress Cataloging-in-Publication Data

Wallace, Holly, 1961-
    Classification / Holly Wallace.
        p. cm. -- (Life processes)
    Includes bibliographical references (p.).
    ISBN 1-57572-337-9 (HC), 1-4034-4073-5 (Pbk.)
     1. Biology--Classification--Juvenile literature. [1. Biology--Classification.] I. Title. II.
    Series.

    QH83 .G26 2000
    570'.1'2--dc21

                                                                    00-040974

Acknowledgments

The author and publishers are grateful to the following for permission to reproduce copyright material: Bruce Coleman/Hans Reinhard, p. 24; Mary Evans Picture Library, p. 4; NHPA/Martin Harvey, pp. 5, 29; NHPA/Laurie Campbell, pp. 6, 9; NHPA/M.I. Walker p. 6; NHPA/Andy Rouse, p. 7; NHPA/ANT, pp. 8, 23; NHPA/Stephen Dalton, pp. 8, 16, 20, 28; NHPA/Alberto Nardi, p. 10; NHPA/E.A. Janes, p. 11; NHPA/Daniel Zupanc, p. 12; NHPA/Anthony Bannister, pp. 13, 15, 28; NHPA/N.A. Callow, p. 14; NHPA/G.I. Bernard, p. 16; NHPA/John Shaw, p. 17; NHPA/Norbert Wu, p. 18; NHPA/Daniel Heuclin, pp. 19, 22, 25; NHPA/LUTRA, p. 21; NHPA/Christophe Ratier, p. 25; NHPA/Nigel J. Dennis, p. 27; Photodisc, pp. 7, 26.

Cover photograph reproduced with permission of NHPA.

Some words are shown in bold, **like this.** You can find out what they mean by looking in the glossary.

Contents

Introduction

Classification explains the system scientists have developed for identifying and naming living things so that a particular **organism** can be recognized all over the world. It also explains how living things are split into groups according to their main characteristics, and describes key examples from the major classification groups.

What Is Classification?

There are amazing numbers of living things on Earth. Scientists use the word **organism** to describe anything that is alive. They also need a way to identify an individual **species** from among the millions of organisms that exist. To do this, they divide living things into groups. This is called classification, or **taxonomy.** It is similar to the system used in a library, where each book is given a code or number to make it easier to find.

Linnaeus's system

The modern system of classification was devised by the Swedish scientist, Carl von Linné (1707–1778). He gave every known living thing a two-part **Latin** name. For example, a tiger is *Panthera tigris*. The two parts work like your last name and first name, to show which family the organism belongs to, and then to identify it as an individual.

Carl von Linné

Latin was used so that the name would be the same all over the world and could be understood by everyone. Von Linné even changed his name to the Latin name Carolus Linnaeus. Today, we use Latin and Latin-like names. The name of the scientist who discovered a new species is often put into a Latin form, and used as part of the name for the species.

Common and scientific names

Many living things have a common name as well as a scientific name. But the same common name might refer to several different organisms. For example, you find badgers in Europe and in the United States. But they are not the same species. Using their scientific names—*Meles meles* for European badger, and *Taxidea taxus* for American badger—avoids any confusion.

4

How does classification work?

Scientists divide living things into groups, based on the features that they have in common. As you move from kingdom to species, the organisms in the group have more in common.

- Kingdoms – all living things divided into five huge groups
- Phyla (singular: phylum) or division – division of one kingdom
- Classes – division of one phylum into smaller groups
- Orders – division of one class into smaller groups
- Families – division of one order into smaller groups
- Genera (singular: genus) – division of one family into small groups that are very similar
- Species – small group made up of organisms that are different from all other groups of living things, and can reproduce together to continue the species

Tiger classification table

This table shows how the *Panthera tigris*, or tiger, is classified.

Kingdom:	Animalia (animals)
Phylum:	Chordata **(chordates)**
Sub-phylum:	Vertebrata **(vertebrates)**
Class:	Mammalia (mammals)
Order:	Carnivora (carnivores)
Family:	Felidae (cats)
Genus:	*Panthera*
Species:	*tigris*

Did you know?

Scientists have no idea exactly how many species of living things exist on Earth. About two million have been described and classified, but the actual number may be ten times higher. New species of plants and animals are discovered each year.

Five Kingdoms

The largest group of classification is the kingdom. At one time, scientists only recognized two kingdoms of living things, the plant kingdom and the animal kingdom. But many **organisms** do not fit into these two groups. They are neither plants nor animals, or they have features of both. Today, we divide living things into five kingdoms.

Moneran kingdom

Monerans are tiny, single-celled organisms like bacteria and blue-green **algae.** They are thought to be one of the most ancient forms of life on Earth. Their cells are very simple and, unlike the cells of all other living things, do not have **nuclei.** There are over 3,000 known **species** of monerans.

Protist kingdom

The protist kingdom is made up of single-celled organisms that have a nucleus and specialized cell parts called **organelles.** There are more than 28,000 known species of protists. All protists live in damp places or in water.

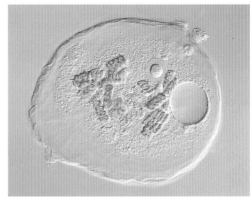

An amoeba is a protist.

Fungi kingdom

Fungi are organisms like molds, mushrooms, and mildew. The body of a fungus is made up of a network of threads called hyphae. Unlike plant cells, hyphae cells do not contain **chlorophyll,** and cannot make their own food by **photosynthesis.** Instead, fungi feed by absorbing food from other organisms, both alive and dead. There are about 75,000 known fungi species.

Fly agaric (*Amanita muscaria*) is a highly poisonous fungus.

Plant kingdom

Plant cells have rigid cell walls made of **cellulose.** Their cells contain a green substance called chlorophyll, which they use to make their own food by photosynthesis. For this they need water and sunlight. Plants do not move from place to place. There are more than 400,000 known plant species.

Animal kingdom

Animals are made up of many cells that form specialized **tissues, organs,** and **organ systems.** Animal cells do not have rigid walls, and they cannot make their own food. Most animals have to move around to find food and escape from danger. There are about 1,500,000 known species of animals.

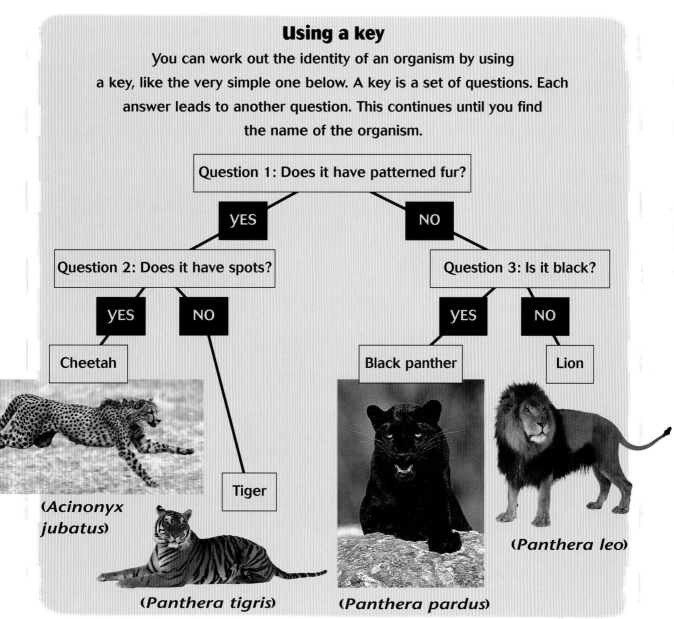

Using a key

You can work out the identity of an organism by using a key, like the very simple one below. A key is a set of questions. Each answer leads to another question. This continues until you find the name of the organism.

Question 1: Does it have patterned fur?

YES

NO

Question 2: Does it have spots?

Question 3: Is it black?

YES

NO

YES

NO

Cheetah

Black panther

Lion

Tiger

(Acinonyx jubatus)

(Panthera tigris)

(Panthera pardus)

(Panthera leo)

Plants without Flowers

The plant kingdom is divided into flowering plants and plants that do not produce flowers. Plants without flowers have been growing on Earth for 300 million years. The prehistoric ancestors of modern horsetails and club mosses grew up to 99 feet (30 meters) tall—higher than a house! Most nonflowering plants grow from tiny, dust-like specks called spores. Thousands of the spores are made, released, and then carried away on the wind. If they land in a suitable place, they will grow into new plants.

Algae

Some biologists classify all types of **algae** as protists. Algae are very simple, nonflowering plants, with no proper roots, leaves, or stems, like the seaweed in the picture. They usually grow in water, and range in size from microscopic, single-celled plants to gigantic seaweeds. They are classified according to their color—red, green, or brown. Plants give off oxygen as waste when they **photosynthesize.** Sea-algae produce about 80 percent of all the **oxygen** in the air.

Mosses and liverworts

Mosses and liverworts are mainly small, ground-hugging plants that live in damp places. They do not have flowers, but produce their spores in a small capsule that is held up on a tiny stalk. When the capsule opens, the spores are carried away on the wind.

The spore capsule of this star moss is ready to release spores into the air.

Ferns, horsetails, and club mosses

Ferns, horsetails, and club mosses also grow from spores. Ferns are plants with frond-like leaves that grow from underground stems. Some have rusty spots under their leaves. These are spore-bearing structures called sporangia.

A monkey puzzle tree is a conifer.

Conifers

Conifers, class Gymnospermae, are trees such as pines, larches, and redwoods. Unlike the other nonflowering plants, they grow new plants from seeds, formed when male **pollen** joins with female **ovules.** But they do not produce flowers. Instead, their pollen, ovules, and seeds grow in woody cones. There are about 550 **species** of conifers.

Did you know?

Lichens are a cross between a fungus and an alga. The alga provides the fungus with food made by photosynthesis. In turn, the fungus protects the alga and provides it with water. It is a highly successful combination. Lichens are extremely tough, and can survive in very cold or hostile conditions.

Simple Plants		Ferns and Horsetails		Conifers	
Kingdom:	Plantae (plants)	Kingdom:	Plantae (plants)	Kingdom:	Plantae (plants)
Division:	Byrophyta (plants with simple roots, stems, and leaves but no **vascular tissue**)	Divisions:	Filicinophyta (ferns); Sphenophyta (horsetails); Lycophyta (club mosses)	Divisions:	Coniferophyta (conifers); Cycadophyta (cycads); Ginkophyta (ginkgoes); Gnetophyta (gnetophytes - tropical and desert shrubs)
Classes:	Hepaticae (liverworts); Musci (mosses); Anthocerotae (hornworts)				

Flowering Plants

Flowering plants belong to the division Anthophyta (angiosperms). Flowers contain the plants' male and female parts, which are needed to make seeds that will grow into new plants. Some flowers have both male and female parts in the same flower, while other plants are either male or female. The male parts make a fine powder called **pollen.** For a seed to grow, the pollen must join with a female **ovule.** This is called **pollination.** Pollen is often carried from flower to flower by the wind or by animals. Flowering plants are by far the biggest group of plants, with about 250,000 **species.** They first grew on Earth about 100 million years ago.

Monocotyledons

Flowering plants can be divided into two classes, monocotyledons and dicotyledons. A cotyledon is a tiny leaf inside a seed. Until the new plant grows its first leaves, it lives off food stored in the cotyledon. Monocotyledons have only one of these leaves in their seeds. The grown plants have narrow leaves with parallel **veins,** and flowers that are divided into three parts. Irises, daffodils, and grasses are monocotyledons.

The poppies (*Papaver* species) in this field are dicotyledons.

Dicotyledons

Dicotyledons have two cotyledons in their seeds. They include plants such as daisies, carrots, cabbages, oak trees, cacti, and roses. Most have broad leaves with a branching pattern of veins. Their flowers are usually divided into four or five parts.

Did you know?

Most types of plants are called vascular plants. This means that they have a system of tiny tubes running through their stems. These tubes are called **vascular tissue** and there are two types, called **xylem** and **phloem.** The xylem carry water from the roots up through the plant. The phloem carry the **sap,** a sugary food made in the leaves, to all parts of the plant. Some nonflowering plants, including **algae,** mosses, and liverworts, do not have vascular tissue.

Trees

Trees are plants with tall, woody trunks instead of stems. The two most common groups of trees are conifers and broadleaved trees. Conifers make seeds but do not make flowers. Broadleaved trees are flowering plants. For example, cherry trees belong to the rose family. Some broadleaved trees are **deciduous.** This means that they lose their leaves once a year.

The leaves of most deciduous trees change color before they fall.

Flowering plant classification	
Kingdom:	Plantae (plants)
Division:	Anthophyta
	(angiosperms, or plants with flowers and fruits)
Classes:	Monocotyledonae
	(monocotyledons, like daffodils and grasses)
	Dicotyledonae
	(dicotyledons, like oak trees and roses)
Number of species:	more than 250,000

Invertebrates

Invertebrates are animals that do not have **vertebrae** or skeletons inside their bodies. With some 950,000 **species,** there are far more invertebrates than **vertebrates** on Earth. About 97 percent of all animal species are invertebrates. They are divided into many different groups, including insects, mollusks, worms, starfish, and jellyfish.

Mollusks

Mollusks make up the second largest group of invertebrates. All mollusks have a soft body that is often protected by a hard shell. Most live in water. Mollusks include snails, like the one in the picture, and slugs, class Gastropoda; clams and mussels, class Bivalvia; and octopuses and squid, class Cephalopoda. Bivalves have two parts to their shells. Cephalopods have a small shell hidden inside their bodies.

Jellyfish and sea anemones

Jellyfish, sea anemones, and corals belong to a group of invertebrates called cnidarians, or phylum Cnidaria. They have soft, circular bodies and mouths surrounded by stinging tentacles used for catching **prey**. All jellyfish can sting, but the box jellyfish of Australia is deadly. Its poison can kill a person within four minutes of being stung!

Worms

Worms, such as earthworms, leeches, and lugworms, are annelids, or phylum Annelida. They have long, tubular bodies divided into segments. The longest earthworm is the giant *Michrochaetus rappi* from South Africa, which grows over three feet (one meter) long. Earthworms spend most of their lives underground. Their burrows help to keep the soil healthy by allowing air and water to circulate through it.

"Spiny-skinned"

Starfish, sea urchins, and their relatives are echinoderms, or phylum Echinodermata. Echinoderm means "spiny-skinned." Echinoderms have chalky skeletons and bodies arranged in five parts. Many starfish, for example, have five arms. If a starfish loses an arm, it can grow another one. Underneath each arm are rows of **tube feet** that the starfish uses to move and to grip its prey.

You can see the bumpy texture characteristic of echinoderms on this starfish and sea urchin.

Invertebrate classification

Kingdom:	Animalia (animals)
Major phyla:	1 Cnidaria (jellyfish)
	2 Echinodermata (starfish)
	3 Platyhelminthes (flatworms)
	4 Nematoda (roundworms)
	5 Mollusca (mollusks)
	6 Annelida (segmented worms)
	7 Arthropoda (arthropods)

Mollusk classification

Kingdom:	Animalia (animals)
Phylum:	Mollusca (mollusks)
Classes:	1 Polyplacophora (chitons)
	2 Gastropoda (snails, slugs)
	3 Bivalvia (clams, mussels)
	4 Cephalopoda (squid, octopuses)
	(plus 3 minor classes)
Number of orders:	about 45
Number of species:	about 75,000

Arthropods

The biggest group of **invertebrates** is the arthropods, or phylum Arthropoda. It includes insects, arachnids, crustaceans, centipedes, and millipedes. With over a million known **species,** it is the largest group of animals on Earth. All arthropods have bodies that are divided into segments and legs that bend at joints. Their soft bodies are covered with hard cases or shells called **exoskeletons.** Most arthropods have **antennae.**

Insect identification

Insects, class Insecta, live all over the world in all types of climate and conditions. All insects have three parts to their bodies—the head, **thorax,** and **abdomen.** They have three pairs of legs attached to the thorax. Most insects have two pairs of wings and can fly. Flies have only one pair of wings, and adult ants and aphids have none. Insects have **compound eyes** made up of hundreds of tiny lenses, and one pair of antennae for smelling, tasting, touching, and sensing vibrations in the air.

Insect classification	
Kingdom:	Animalia (animals)
Phylum:	Arthropoda (arthropods)
Sub-phylum:	Uniramia (one pair of antennae)
Class:	Insecta (insects)
Number of orders:	19
Number of species:	about 1 million

Honeybees (*Apis mellifera*) are typical insects.

Crustaceans

Like insects, crustaceans, or sub-phylum Crustacea, are arthropods. Most of the 44,000 species of crustaceans live in the ocean. Woodlice, class Isopoda, are unusual because they live on land. Crustaceans have bodies divided into many segments, each with a pair of jointed legs for walking and swimming. They have two pairs of antennae, and most are covered in hard shells. Crustaceans include crabs, lobsters, barnacles, water fleas, shrimps, and woodlice.

Centipedes and millipedes

Centipedes, class Chilopoda, and millipedes, class Diplopoda, are myriapods, or "many-legged" arthropods. Both have long, many-segmented bodies and, from a distance, they look alike. But centipedes have one pair of legs on each body segment, while millipedes have two. Millipedes, like the one in the picture, are plant-eaters, while centipedes are fierce **predators**, paralyzing their **prey** with poison fangs.

There are about 11,000 known species of centipedes and millipedes.

Did you know?

There are more different kinds of insects than all other species of animal put together. According to some experts, nearly 90 percent of all animals are insects. At least one million species have already been described, and scientists are finding new species all the time, at the rate of about 8,000 to 10,000 species a year. There may be another 30 million species waiting to be found!

Arachnids

Spiders and their relatives, the scorpions, ticks, and mites, make up the class of animals called arachnids. Like insects, arachnids are **invertebrates.** Arachnids are also arthropods. There are important differences between insects and arachnids. Arachnids have only two parts to their bodies—the **cephalothorax,** consisting of the head and thorax joined together, and a large **abdomen.** They have four pairs of legs and do not have wings or **antennae.**

Spider spinners

Spiders, of the order Araneae, are famous for their silk-making skills. The silk is made inside the spider's body and squeezed out through tiny nozzles, called spinnerets, at its rear. Some spiders weave silk webs to catch their **prey.** Others are hunters, chasing their prey on the ground. Once the prey is caught, the spider bites and kills it with its poison fangs. There are about 35,000 known **species** of spiders, with perhaps as many as 200,000 still waiting to be discovered.

This huge tropical spider has killed a tree frog.

Sting in the tail

Scorpions, order Scorpionida, have a distinctive appearance, as you can see in the picture. Like spiders, they have four pairs of legs. They also have a pair of strong, pincher-like claws, used for grabbing prey. Many scorpions have poisonous stingers in their tails that they mainly use in self-defense. There are about 800 known species of scorpions.

Ticks and mites

Ticks and mites, order Acari, are **parasites,** living on other animals and plants, and feeding on their sap, blood, fur, or feathers. Some common mites live on household dust that is mostly made up of flakes of dead human skin! Most ticks and mites are very tiny—smaller than a grain of rice. But they can be deadly, spreading diseases in humans, animals, and food crops. There are about 30,000 known species of ticks and mites.

This wood tick is sucking human blood.

Arachnid classification	
Kingdom:	Animalia (animals)
Phylum:	Arthropoda (arthropods)
Sub-phylum:	Chelicerata (chelicerates, animals with pincher-like mouthparts)
Class:	Arachnida (arachnids)
Number of orders:	11
Number of species:	about 75,000

Fish

Fish are **vertebrates.** There are as many **species** of fish as all other vertebrates—amphibians, reptiles, birds, and mammals—put together. Fish are **cold-blooded.** They live in both freshwater and saltwater, and breathe in oxygen through **gills.** Fish are designed for swimming, with muscular, streamlined bodies often covered in scales, and with fins instead of limbs. Fish were the earliest known vertebrates on Earth. The first fish appeared about 515 million years ago.

Rubbery skeletons

Sharks, rays, and skates belong to the group of **cartilaginous** fish, or class Chondrichthyes. Instead of bone, they have skeletons made of rubbery, flexible **cartilage.** They also have a series of separate gill slits along each side of the body. With its razor-sharp teeth and man-eating reputation, the most famous shark is the great white. But the largest shark is the enormous whale shark that feeds on **plankton** filtered from the water. This giant can grow up to 60 feet (18 meters) long, but it is harmless.

Caribbean reef sharks (*Carcharhinus perezi*) are cartilaginous fish.

Bony fish

More than 95 percent of all fish are bony fish, or class Osteichthyes. As their name suggests, bony fish have skeletons made of bone. Their gills are covered by a flap with a single opening at the rear. This group includes herrings, salmon, angler fish, eels, and carp. It is found all over the world, from vast oceans to tiny ponds. The longest bony fish is the striking-looking oarfish. It can grow over 30 feet (9 meters) long, and it looks like a silvery ribbon, with a long, red fin down its back.

How fish breathe

Fish use their gills to breathe **oxygen** dissolved in the water. As a fish swims, it is opening and closing its mouth. As it opens its mouth, it gulps in water. As it closes its mouth, it pushes the water out through its gills. As the water passes over the gills, the fish's blood vessels absorb oxygen from the water and release waste carbon dioxide into the water to be pushed out.

Did you know?

Despite its strange, S-shaped body, the seahorse is a true fish. It belongs to the same group as sticklebacks and pipefish, order Gasterosteiformes. Seahorses are weak, slow swimmers, using their delicate back fins to move. They are often seen clinging to seaweed with their tails to avoid having to swim at all.

Seahorses (*Hippocampus hippocampus*) are really fish.

Fish classification	
Kingdom:	Animalia (animals)
Phylum:	Chordata **(chordates)**
Sub-phylum:	Vertebrata **(vertebrates)**
Classes:	1 Lampreys and hagfish (jawless fish)
	2 Chondrichthyes (fish with skeletons made of cartilage)
	3 Osteichthyes (fish with skeletons made of bone)
Number of orders:	20
Number of species:	about 24,000 (with about 100 new species discovered every year)

Amphibians

The ancestors of modern amphibians were the first **vertebrates** to leave the water to search for food and to live on land. They first appeared on Earth about 370 million years ago. Amphibians are **cold-blooded** vertebrates. They have smooth, scaleless skin. Their young breathe through **gills,** like fish. Adult amphibians have lungs, but they also breathe through their skins, which they must keep moist to absorb **oxygen** properly.

Frogs and toads

Frogs and toads belong to the order Anura. They look similar, but there are several ways of telling them apart. Frogs, like the one in the picture, have smoother skin and longer legs for jumping. Toads have lumpy warts on their skins and squatter bodies. Most frogs and toads live on or near the ground, and feed on fast-moving **prey** such as insects and spiders. There are about 3,800 known **species** of frogs and toads, or anurans, living all over the world. About 20 new species are discovered each year.

The name amphibian comes from a Greek word *amphibios*, which means "a being with a double life." This describes the way amphibians live both in water and on land. Most amphibians spend their adult lives on land. But they must return to the water to breed and to lay their eggs.

Newts and salamanders

Newts and salamanders belong to the order Urodela, or Caudata. They live in the damp undergrowth near water, and feed on **invertebrates** such as slugs, snails, and worms. They have longer bodies and shorter legs than anurans, and long, distinctive tails. When a newt or salamander loses a leg or a part of its tail, it can grow a new one. There are about 360 known species of newts and salamanders.

The salamander's long tail helps it balance and swim.

Caecilians

Caecilians belong to the third order of amphibians, Gymnophiona. Their long, cylindrical shape makes them look more like earthworms than amphibians. Caecilians do not have legs. They are nearly blind, and live in water or burrow in soft earth, feeding on earthworms and other invertebrates. There are about 170 known species of caecilians, all living in tropical climates. Most are about 20 inches (50 centimeters) long, but some are up to 5 feet (1.5 meters) long!

Amphibian classification	
Kingdom:	Animalia (animals)
Phylum:	Chordata (**chordates**)
Sub-phylum:	Vertebrata (**vertebrates**)
Class:	Amphibia (amphibians)
Number of orders:	3
Number of species:	about 4,500

Reptiles

Snakes, lizards, crocodiles, and turtles are all types of reptile. Reptiles are **vertebrates.** Because they are **cold-blooded,** they usually live in warm places where the sun heats their bodies and makes them active. Reptiles are much better adapted for life on land than amphibians. Their scaly skin protects their bodies and keeps them from drying out, and they lay eggs protected by tough, leathery shells. Some reptiles give birth to live young. There are about 6,500 known **species** of reptiles, divided into four main orders.

Snakes and lizards

With about 6,000 species, snakes and lizards, of order Squamata, form the largest group of reptiles. Although snakes look quite different from lizards, scientists believe that they evolved from lizard-like ancestors that had two pairs of legs. Lizards range in size from tiny geckos, family Gekkonidae, to the huge Komodo dragon, or *Varanus komodoensis*, of Indonesia. The longest snake in the world is the reticulated python, *Python reticulatus*, of Southeast Asia, which can grow up to 30 feet (10 meters) long.

This red spitting cobra is protecting her eggs.

Alligators and crocodiles

Alligators and crocodiles, order Crocodilia, are the largest living reptiles. These giants are covered in large, hard scales, strengthened with bone. They are well adapted for life in water, using their powerful tails for swimming. Their eyes and nostrils are on top of their heads so that they can lie submerged in water but still see and breathe. Crocodilians are fierce **predators.** They drag **prey** under water and tear it apart with their sharp, pointed teeth.

Turtles and tortoises

Turtles, tortoises, and terrapins make up the order Chelonia. They have bony shells for protection and beak-like jaws instead of teeth. They live in oceans, in rivers, and on land, and feed on plants and small animals. Some turtles and tortoises can live for a very long time. One Marion's tortoise lived to be 152 years old.

Reptile classification	
Kingdom:	Animalia (animals)
Phylum:	Chordata **(chordates)**
Subphylum:	Vertebrata **(vertebrates)**
Class:	Reptilia (reptiles)
Number of orders:	4 (major)
Number of species:	about 6,500

Did you know?

The tuatara, *Sphenodon punctatus*, is the only living member of an ancient order of reptiles called Rhynchocephalia. Its ancestors appeared about 220 million years ago, before the first dinosaurs. Today, tuataras are only found in New Zealand. Their name comes from a local word meaning "peaks on the back", which refers to the spiky crest growing along the tuatara's back and tail.

Birds

Birds are **warm-blooded vertebrates.** They are the only animals whose bodies are covered with feathers. Most birds can fly. Birds breathe air through lungs. They have beaks but no teeth, and produce their young by laying eggs with hard shells. Birds are found all over the world, in cities, in steamy rain forests, and at the icy poles. They range in size from the huge African ostrich, *Struthio camelus*, which stands 7 feet (2 meters) tall, to tiny bee hummingbirds, *Mellisuga helenae*, from Central America, that are no bigger than butterflies.

Perching birds

The largest order of birds is the order Passeriformes, called perching birds. It includes over 5,500 **species,** almost 60 percent of all known birds. Passerines have four toes on their feet, three pointing forwards and one pointing backwards, for gripping branches.

Bird classification	
Kingdom:	Animalia (animals)
Phylum:	Chordata (chordates)
Subphylum:	Vertebrata (vertebrates)
Class:	Aves (birds)
Number of orders:	23
Number of species:	more than 8,500

The painted bunting (*Passerina ciris*) is a perching bird.

Did you know?

The first bird lived on Earth about 150 million years ago. It was given the **Latin** name *Archaeopteryx,* which means "ancient wings." Fossils found in the 1860s show that it was about the size of a pigeon, with feathers, wings, and a wishbone in its skeleton, like a modern bird. But it also had teeth and a long, bony tail, like a reptile. From creatures like *Archaeopteryx*, scientists have been able to show that birds are the living descendants of dinosaurs.

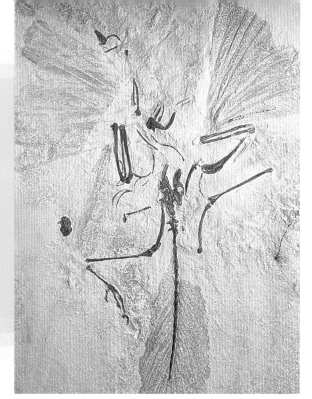

This *Archaeopteryx* fossil was found in Germany.

Flightless birds

Some birds, including ostriches and penguins, have wings but cannot fly. Ostriches, order Struthioniformes, are the largest birds in the world. They are too heavy to fly but can run faster than a racehorse, at more than 40 miles per hour (70 kilometers per hour). Penguins, order Sphenisciformes, look clumsy on land but seem to fly under water! Using its wings as flippers, the gentoo penguin can reach speeds of about 25 miles per hour (40 kilometers per hour), which is three times faster than the fastest human swimmer!

The ostrich (*Struthio camelus*) is a flightless bird.

25

Mammals

There are more than 4,000 **species** of mammals, ranging from huge elephants and whales to tiny bats and shrews. Human beings also belong to the mammal class. Mammals are **warm-blooded vertebrates** that breathe air using lungs. They are the only animals to produce milk, which they use to feed their young. They also look after their young until they are old enough to fend for themselves. Mammals are the only animals with outer ears, used to channel sound down into their ears.

Marsupials

Marsupials, order Marsupiala, are mammals with pouches. They include kangaroos, koalas, and wombats. Their newborn young are very tiny and weak. After birth, they crawl into their mother's pouch, where they feed on milk and grow.

Kangaroos are marsupials.

Monotremes

Three species of mammal, the duck-billed platypus, the long-beaked echidna, and the short-beaked echidna, belong to the order Monotremata. Monotremes are mammals that lay eggs. A female duck-billed platypus, *Ornithorhynchus anatinus*, lays her soft, sticky eggs in a riverbank tunnel. When the eggs hatch, she feeds her young on milk like other mammals.

Mammal classification	
Kingdom:	Animalia (animals)
Phylum:	Chordata **(chordates)**
Subphylum:	Vertebrata (vertebrates)
Class:	Mammalia (mammals)
Subclasses:	1 Prototheria (egg-laying)
	2 Theria (do not lay eggs)
Infraclasses:	1 Eutheria **(placental)**
	2 Metatheria (non-placental)
Number of orders:	19
Number of species:	more than 4,000

Mammal orders

Order	Examples	No. Species
Artiodacytyla	Camels, pigs, cattle	**ca.** 180
Carnivora	Cats, bears, dogs	ca. 250
Cetacea	Whales, dolphins	72
Chiroptera	Bats	ca. 800
Dermoptera	Flying lemurs	2
Edentata	Anteaters, sloths	29
Hyracoidea	Hyraxes	ca. 6
Insectivora	Moles, shrews	ca. 350
Lagomorpha	Rabbits, hares	ca. 60
Marsupiala	Kangaroos, koalas	ca. 275
Monotremata	Platypus, spiny anteater	3
Perissodactyla	Tapirs, rhinos, horses	15
Pholidota	Pangolins	7
Pinnipedia	Seals, sea lions, walrus	34
Primates	Lemurs, monkeys, humans	ca. 200
Proboscidea	Elephants	2
Rodentia	Mice, porcupines, beavers	ca. 1,750
Sirenia	Dugongs, manatees	4
Tubulidentata	Aardvark	1

Did you know?

The aardvark, *Orycteropus afer*, is the only living member of its order, Tubulidentata. This unusual, ant-eating mammal lives in the **grasslands** of Africa. Its body is specialized for burrowing after its food with long, spade-shaped claws, and powerful back legs. Instead of running away from enemies, the aardvark digs a hole and hides. As it digs, it folds back its ears and closes its nostrils to keep soil out.

More Mammals

Most mammals are **placental** mammals. Their babies grow inside the mothers' bodies until they are fully formed. They receive nourishment from their mother through her placenta, and when they are born, they look like smaller versions of their parents. Placental mammals include whales, bats, and human beings.

Flying mammals

Bats, order Chiroptera, make up nearly a quarter of all mammal **species.** Bats, like the one in the picture, are the only mammals that can truly fly, although some mammals can glide. The name

Chiroptera is **Latin** for "hand-wings." This is because a bat's wings have evolved from its hands and arms. Its finger bones are very long, with leathery skin stretched between them. The wings are also attached to the bat's back legs and tail. There are two main groups of bat—large fruit bats, or flying foxes, and smaller insect-eaters.

Did you know?

The African elephant, *Loxodonta africana*, is the world's largest living land mammal. An adult male elephant can weigh more than 6 tons (5 tonnes) and stand 9 feet (3 meters) tall. Incredibly, their closest mammal relative is believed to be the rabbit-sized hyrax, order *Hyracoidea*. Hyrax and elephants originated from the same mammal group 55 million years ago.

These hyraxes are closely related to the elephant.

Sea mammals

There are about 120 species of sea mammals, belonging to three orders—Cetacea, whales and dolphins; Pinnipedia, seals, sea lions, and walruses; and Sirenia, dugongs and manatees. They include the gigantic blue whale, the largest mammal that has ever lived. Blue whales, *Balaenoptera musculus*, can weigh 143 tons (130 tonnes) and grow more than 98 feet (30 meters) long.

Human mammals

Human beings, *Homo sapiens*, belong to the order of primates. There are about 200 species of primates, divided into two groups. The anthropoids include apes—chimpanzees, gorillas, orangutans and gibbons—monkeys, and humans. Humans are very closely related to apes. Gorillas and chimpanzees are more closely related to us than they are to orangutans. The prosimians include galagos and lemurs.

Chimpanzees are closely related to humans.

Human classification	
Kingdom:	Animalia (animals)
Phylum:	Chordata (chordates)
Subphylum:	Vertebrata (vertebrates)
Class:	Mammalia (mammals)
Subclass:	Eutheria (placental)
Order:	Primates (primates)
Family:	Hominidae (homonids)
Species:	*Homo sapiens* (humans)

Conclusion

Think how difficult it would be to find the book you wanted in a bookstore or library if the books were all mixed together. Organizing them according to subject, author, or title makes them much easier to find. This is why classification is so useful for identifying living things. Once you know the scientific name of a plant or animal, you can find out what it is, and how it is related to other living things.

Glossary

abdomen   end part of an insect's or arachnid's body

algae   one-celled plant found in both saltwater and freshwater

antenna   feeler-like part on an insect's head, used for touching, sensing changes in temperature, and detecting tastes and smells

breed   to have babies

ca.   abbreviation for circa, meaning approximately

cartilage   rubbery, flexible tissue

cartilaginous   something made of cartilage

cellulose   tough material made of fibers, found in plant cell walls

cephalothorax   front part of an arachnid's body, with the head and thorax joined together

chlorophyll   green coloring found inside plant cells that absorbs energy from sunlight for use in photosynthesis

chordate   living thing that at some time in its life has a stiff, skeletal rod of cells supporting the spinal cord

cold-blooded   animals, including fish, amphibians, and reptiles, that cannot control their own body temperature, and rely on the weather to warm them up or cool them down

compound eye   special eye made up of hundreds of tiny, individual lenses

deciduous   trees and plants that regularly shed their leaves

exoskeleton   tough, outer coat or shell that insects or crabs have to protect and support their soft bodies

gills   thin, feathery body part that fish use for breathing

grassland   large, open, flat area covered in grasses and low bushes

infraclasses   two special subclasses found only in mammals

invertebrates   animals that do not have backbones or skeletons inside their bodies

Latin   language originally spoken in ancient Rome, used in science to describe living things

nucleus   rounded structure inside a cell that is the cell's control center

organism   scientific word for a living thing

organ   group of tissues in a living thing's body that work together to do a certain job

organelle   parts in a cell that have a special job to do

organ system   group of organs working together in a living thing's body

ovule   female sex cell of a plant—after fertilization it becomes a seed

oxygen   gas that all living things need to take in to survive

parasite plant or animal that lives on or in other plants or animals and gets all its food from them

phloem tubes that carry food through a plant

photosynthesis process by which green plants make food from carbon dioxide and water, using energy from sunlight absorbed by their chlorophyll

placental mammal that has young that develop inside the mother's bodies until they are fully formed

plankton tiny plants and animals that live in water and provide food for many other animals

pollen tiny grains that are the male sex cells of plants

pollination transfer of pollen from a male flower to a female flower or from male to female parts of a flower

predator animal that hunts and kills other animals for food

prey animal that is hunted and eaten by other animals

sap liquid in a plant that carries food and water

species group of living things grouped together because they have similar features and can breed with each other

spore tiny, dust-like speck produced by fungi and many other nonflowering plants that grows into a new plant

taxonomy way that living things are divided into groups, based on the features they have in common, to make them easier to identify and study—also called classification

thorax the middle part of an insect's body bearing the legs and wings

tissue group of cells in a living thing's body that have a special job to do, like bone and muscle

tube feet tiny, tube-like tentacles that starfish and other echinoderms use for breathing, moving, and grasping food

vascular tissue system of tubes that carries water and sap around a plant

veins **1)** tiny tubes in a leaf that carry food and water **2)** vessels that carry blood to the heart

vertebrae interlinked bones in a backbone

vertebrates animals with backbones and skeletons inside their bodies, including fish, amphibians, reptiles, birds, and mammals

warm-blooded animals that can control their own body temperature so that it stays the same no matter how hot or cold it is

xylem tubes that carry food through a plant

More Books to Read

Anderson, Margaret Jean. *Carl Linnaeus: Father of Classification.* Berkeley Heights, N.J.: Enslow Publishers, 1997.

Greenaway, Theresa. *The Plant Kingdom: A Guide to Plant Classification & Biodiversity.* Austin, Tex.: Raintree Steck-Vaughn Publishers, 1999.

Whyman, Kathryn. *The Animal Kingdom: A Guide to Vertebrate Classification & Biodiversity.* Austin, Tex.: Raintree Steck-Vaughn Publishers, 1999.

Index